STONEWALL

A BUILDING.
AN UPRISING.
A REVOLUTION.

written by Rob Sanders

illustrated by Jamey Christoph

Random House New York

Text copyright © 2019 by Rob Sanders
Jacket art and interior illustrations copyright © 2019 by Jamey Christoph

All rights reserved. Published in the United States by Random House Children's Books,
a division of Penguin Random House LLC, New York.

Random House and the colophon are registered trademarks of Penguin Random House LLC.

Visit us on the Web! rhcbooks.com

Educators and librarians, for a variety of teaching tools, visit us at RHTeachersLibrarians.com

Library of Congress Cataloging-in-Publication Data
Names: Sanders, Rob, author. | Christoph, Jamey, illustrator.
Title: Stonewall : A building. An uprising. A revolution. / by Rob Sanders ; illustrated by Jamey Christoph.
Description: First edition. | New York : Random House, [2019]
Identifiers: LCCN 2017013327 (print) | LCCN 2017030919 (ebook) |
ISBN 978-1-5247-1952-4 (hc) | ISBN 978-1-5247-1953-1 (glb) | ISBN 978-1-5247-1954-8 (ebk)
Subjects: LCSH: Stonewall Riots, New York, N.Y., 1969—Juvenile literature. |
Gay rights—United States—History—20th century—Juvenile literature. |
Gays—United States—History—20th century—Juvenile literature.
Classification: LCC HQ76.8.U5 (ebook) | LCC HQ76.8.U5 S26 2019 (print) |
DDC 323.3/264097470904—dc23

Book design by Nicole de las Heras

MANUFACTURED IN CHINA
10 9 8 7 6 5 4 3 2 1
First Edition

With gratitude to my Nashville family,
who helped me stand up and come out
—R.S.

For Brad—
my love, my best friend, my world
—J.C.

Special thanks to
Andrew Berman, Martin Boyce, David Carter, Lillian Faderman,
Rebecca Kling, E. Patrick Johnson, Ken Lustbader, and Eric Marcus
for their generous help and support of this project and for ensuring
that we will always have a path back to Stonewall

Two stable houses, side by side.

For more than a hundred years, we witnessed history.

Then came a night when we became part of history.

We were built in the 1840s to board the horses of the affluent in New York City's Greenwich Village.

Inside our brick walls, horses whinnied and hammers clanged.

Outside, passersby bustled as carriages rumbled on the cobblestone streets.

As time passed, the wealthy residents began to move uptown, taking with them their art clubs, libraries, fine hotels, and theaters.

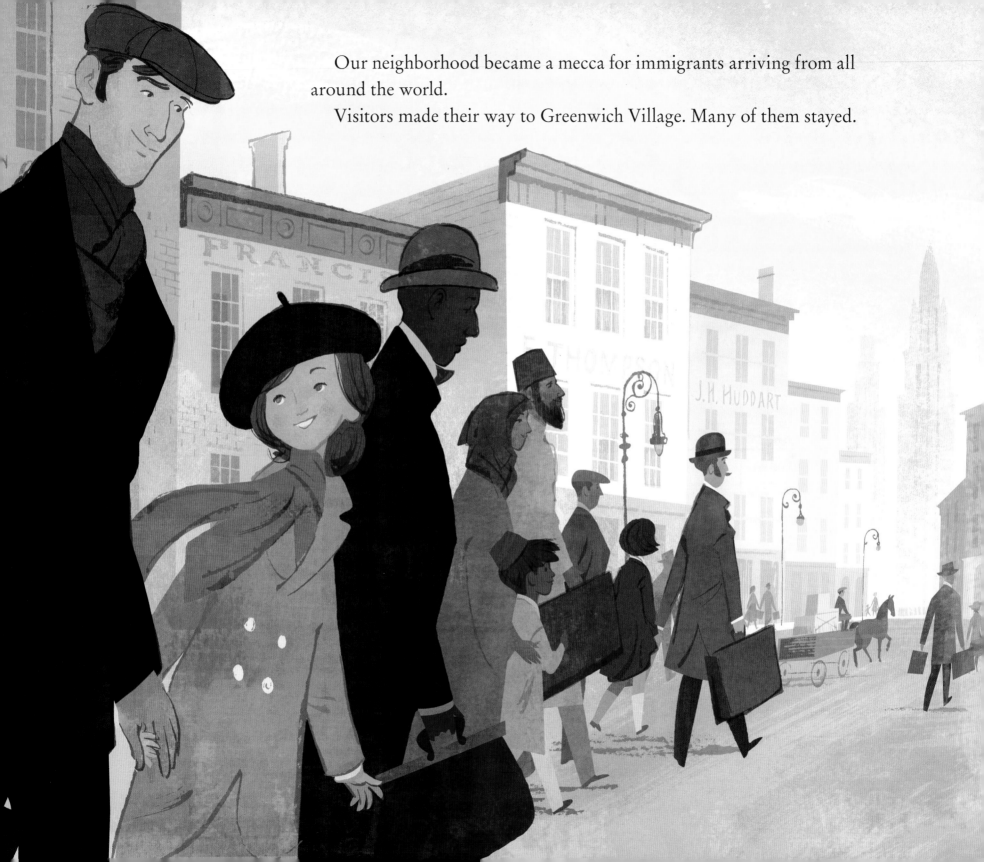

Our neighborhood became a mecca for immigrants arriving from all around the world.

Visitors made their way to Greenwich Village. Many of them stayed.

Greenwich Village was changing.
We changed, too. The smell of
freshly baked bread began to waft out
our windows and into the neighborhood.

The roar of automobiles replaced the rumble
of carriages as artists and writers moved in.
Contemporary-art galleries, experimental theaters,
and small restaurants sprang up around us.
The Village was becoming the creative center
of New York City.

By 1930, our two buildings were joined together, and we became Bonnie's Stone Wall restaurant. Celebrities, artisans, tourists, and local residents lunched at our tables, shoulder to shoulder.

Greenwich Village was a place where you could be yourself,
and where being different was welcomed and accepted.

CHRISTOPHER ST

Newness thumped in the heart of Greenwich Village in the 1950s, vibrating our windows. Musicians played on the streets. Jazz filled the air.

Poets performed in restaurants.

Artists painted in their studios.

The Beat movement arrived,
and we witnessed it all.

Leading up to the 1960s, our neighborhood welcomed gays and lesbians—men who loved men, and women who loved women. We were a home for people who were told that they didn't fit in or belong.

We had welcomed all kinds of people before, so we knew what to do. In 1967, we swung open our doors and became the Stonewall Inn. Gay men and women from throughout the city and the country came to meet old and new friends, free to be themselves inside our walls.

Women and men, young and old, teenagers, transgender people, drag queens, veterans, businesspeople, students, people of different colors, religions, and cultures, gathered, chatted, laughed, and danced under our roof.

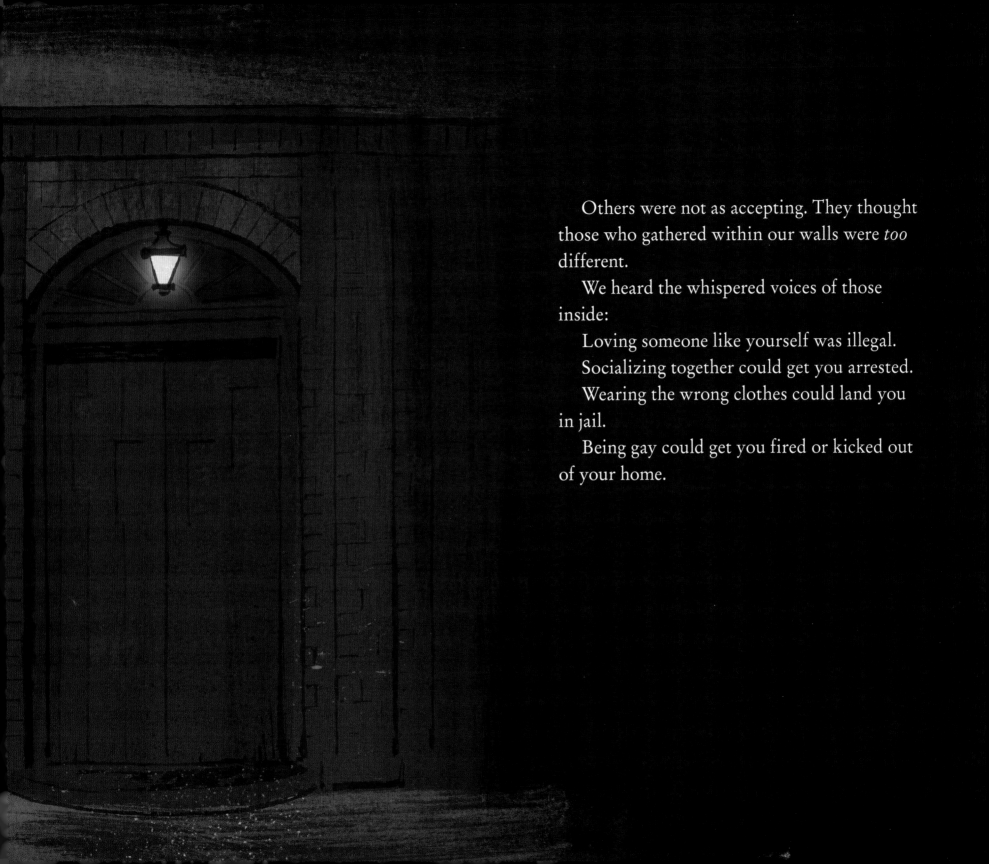

Others were not as accepting. They thought those who gathered within our walls were *too* different.

We heard the whispered voices of those inside:

Loving someone like yourself was illegal.

Socializing together could get you arrested.

Wearing the wrong clothes could land you in jail.

Being gay could get you fired or kicked out of your home.

Some nights, we heard fists pounding on our doors, felt angry footsteps stomping across our floor, and saw flashes of glaring light as the police arrested some of those inside.

After each raid, those who hadn't been arrested left quietly, angrily, disappearing into the darkness.
We stood tall and kept opening our doors. People kept coming.

But the police raids kept coming, too.
We couldn't stop them.
In the steaming early-morning hours of June 28, 1969,
under a nearly full moon, another raid began.

THIS IS A
RAIDED
PREMISES

POLICE DEP'T.
CITY OF NEW YORK
...RD P. LEARY, POLICE COMMISSIONER

"Police!" a voice shouted. "We're taking the place!"

Officers stormed through our doors, lining up the people inside, demanding IDs, detaining some, arresting others.

This time, those not arrested didn't disappear into the night. Instead, they stood defiantly in the street and on the sidewalk under our rusty sign.

This time, they weren't quiet.

As the ones arrested were led to police cars and patrol wagons, the anger of the growing crowd was lit.

"Why don't you do something?" yelled one woman as she was forced into a police car.

Immediately, the spark of anger grew into a smoldering resistance.

Shouts and screams echoed off bricks. Fists thrust in the air.

We saw the faces of the crowd, and felt their rage.

The Stonewall Uprising had begun.

The police, shocked by the defiance of the crowd, rushed back in and barricaded themselves inside.

Our friends stood outside, trying to force open our doors. Our windows were shattered. Smoke drifted through our rooms. We stood firm.

Years of silent anger inflamed the crowd.

The police called for help, and it soon arrived.

The fires were extinguished. The police came back outside.

But the crowd's anger was *not* extinguished.

"Gay power!" the protestors shouted. "We want freedom!"

The police had never seen anything like it before.

Neither had we.

And it wasn't over. The Stonewall Uprising continued on and off for several days and nights.

A new day was dawning for the gay rights movement.* The change had begun *here*, inside *our* walls, at the Stonewall Inn.

*Now known as the LGBTQ+ rights movement.

On June 28, 1970, our windows looked out on men and women gathering to celebrate the first anniversary of the Stonewall Uprising.

At first, hundreds marched. Then thousands of women and men, young and old, teenagers, transgender people, drag queens, veterans, businesspeople, students, people of different colors, religions, and cultures, *and* their friends and families joined to parade through the streets of New York City.

"Say it clear, say it loud. Gay is good, gay is proud," they chanted.

Many things *are* different now.

Some things *have* changed.

Even some laws have changed.

Now two men who love each other, or two women who love each other, can marry.

We know. We've seen their happy faces snapping photos outside our door. We've heard their footsteps walking side by side along our floors. We've felt their love.

Each year in June, people all over the world celebrate the movement for LGBTQ+ rights—a movement that has come so far—a movement that still has further to go. They celebrate inside and outside our walls. They celebrate freedom. They celebrate equality.

It all began one night here at the Stonewall Inn, when two old horse stables became part of history.

An exterior shot of the
Stonewall Inn, 1969.

THE HISTORY OF THE STONEWALL INN

Originally, the Stonewall Inn's building was a pair of two-story stable houses that were built in 1843 and 1846 at what is now 51–53 Christopher Street, Greenwich Village, New York City. Over the years, the buildings were changed many times. In 1930, the two were joined to form Bonnie's Stone Wall restaurant, and by the 1950s, it became the Stonewall Inn Restaurant. More renovations began in 1966, and it reopened the next year as the Stonewall Inn, a bar and dance club for the gay community.

Police raids were common at gay clubs, and patrons were routinely harassed and arrested for being there, for what they wore, and for not carrying identification. Early in the morning of June 28, 1969, New York City police officers again raided the Stonewall Inn, arresting thirteen people—but not without resistance from those in the crowd. The group at the Stonewall Inn that night represented a diverse cross section of people—those who were gay, lesbian, transgender, drag queens, people of different colors and religions, teenage street kids, businesspeople, and others. The term *transgender* was not used as widely in the 1960s as it is today, but transgender individuals were instrumental in the Uprising, with some historians saying that trans women of color led it.

News of the first night of resistance spread, and more protests and unrest followed. Because not everyone had the same view from the crowd, people there that night have told different accounts of how it all began. Our view of history can depend on where we were standing. The American gay rights movement—now known as the LGBTQ+ rights movement—took a giant step forward that night through the collective efforts of the diverse crowd gathered at the Stonewall Inn.

On June 23, 1992, a sculpture celebrating the Stonewall Uprising was unveiled across from the Stonewall Inn at Christopher Park. American artist George Segal created the work, entitled *Gay Liberation*.

In March 2000, the Stonewall Inn was named a National Historic Landmark, and in 2016, President Barack Obama designated the inn and part of the surrounding neighborhood as the first national monument honoring the LGBTQ+ community.

An iconic image of the clash between police and protestors during the Uprising.

After the initial Uprising, a group of young people gather outside the boarded-up Stonewall Inn.

The famous red neon sign that now hangs in the window of the Stonewall Inn.

From left to right: trans activists Sylvia Ray Rivera and Marsha P. Johnson and lesbian activists Barbara Deming and Kady van Deurs stand outside New York City Hall during a gay rights rally in 1973.

Some of the damage caused in the Uprising was to the Stonewall Inn's jukebox and chairs.

A sign the police once hung at the Stonewall Inn is now framed, and one of the first things visitors see when they walk in.

A group of activists march in Times Square in 1969.

AN INTERVIEW WITH MARTIN BOYCE

Stonewall Uprising Participant and LGBTQ+ Activist

WHAT WAS THE ATMOSPHERE OF THE WEST VILLAGE LIKE IN 1969?

The Village was known as a sanctuary for all social outcasts. It was safe in the day, although the night posed some hazards because the Village was a hot spot attracting an unpredictable crowd. All in all, it was a comfortable place.

WHAT WAS IT LIKE INSIDE THE STONEWALL?

There wasn't even running water behind the bar. We didn't expect much in those times. But the Stonewall had a good dancing space, great music, and an army of interesting characters. It was amazing!

ON THE NIGHT OF THE UPRISING, WHEN DID YOU REALIZE THE CROWD WASN'T GOING TO BACK DOWN?

When the raid ended, we had formed a semicircle around the Stonewall with the police directly in front of us. The Uprising started at the same time, but in different sections, depending on the verbal provocations of the police. In my section, the cop confidently began verbally harassing us and said to leave, and then turned his back to us. But we didn't leave. Instead, we slowly moved ourselves toward him. He forcefully turned around with a face full of rage to repeat the order, but he didn't get a chance to. He looked into our eyes, gulped, blinked, and headed for safety inside the Stonewall. The Uprising was on!

WHAT IS ONE OF YOUR MOST VIVID MEMORIES OF THE UPRISING?

All of a sudden, in the middle of the chaos, there was a brief, eerie quiet, followed by the sound of stomping boots. The crowd opened up, and there they were—the riot police—with clubs, body shields, and all the rest. They stopped and stared at a particular motley group of gays who had formed a chorus line of dancers, kicking their legs Rockettes-style. The police were stunned.

AS IT WAS HAPPENING, DID YOU HAVE ANY IDEA HOW IMPORTANT THIS WOULD BECOME HISTORICALLY?

Not historically, but locally. There was a change in gay people in New York City. In the community, there was finally more a feeling of confidence than shame. Gays were actually proud of what we had done. We proved we could stand up for ourselves! It's also important to note the role of lesbians that night. It was not their bar, but they were there with us. The story of Stonewall is incomplete without realizing this aspect. We made this march to freedom arm in arm.

BEFORE YOU GOT HOME AFTER THE UPRISING, YOUR FATHER HEARD ABOUT IT ON THE RADIO. WHAT DID HE SAY TO YOU?

My father had been a taxi driver since 1933. He was also a rebel. An Anglo-American Catholic, he married my mother, who was Sicilian, and that had raised eyebrows in his family. He was always sympathetic to outsiders. My father had seen much oppression from his cab. He said, "It's about time you people did something." Yes, we were a people!

WHAT IS A PIECE OF ADVICE YOU WOULD GIVE TO YOUNG ACTIVISTS?

I have always regarded the word *Stonewall* as a verb, an action word. It made all gays potential activists. The LGBTQ+ movement has taken flight on the wings of youth. Activism takes so many forms. There is a quote I always remember: "I think. That is how I fight." And fight we must!

GLOSSARY

arrested: being taken into custody by the police

Beat movement: an American social and literary movement beginning in the 1950s

bisexual: someone who is attracted to both males and females

drag queen: a man who dresses in women's clothing, often to perform or entertain

equality: the state of being equal

freedom: the state of being free or at liberty

gay: a person who loves and is attracted to a person of the same gender

ID: a form of identification, such as a driver's license

immigrants: people who move to another country

lesbian: a female who loves and is attracted to other women

LGBTQ+: an acronym for *lesbian, gay, bisexual, transgender, queer, and questioning,* with the *T* also representing transsexual and two-spirit individuals

queer: a term for sexual and gender minorities

raid: a sudden invasion by the police

resistance: the act of resisting or opposing

transgender: when a person knows they are different than the gender they were thought to be at birth

uprising: the act of rising up, revolting, or rioting

FOR FURTHER READING

WEBSITES
LGBT History of Greenwich Village
(gvshp.org/lesbianandgayhistory.htm)

New York Public Library, Diana Davies Photographs
(digitalcollections.nypl.org/collections/diana-davies-photographs)

NYC LGBT Historic Sites Project
(nyclgbtsites.org)

Stonewall National Monument
(nps.gov/ston)

BOOKS
A Is for Activist by Innosanto Nagara

Gay & Lesbian History for Kids: The Century-Long Struggle for LGBT Rights by Jerome Pohlen

Peaceful Fights for Equal Rights by Rob Sanders, illustrated by Jared Andrew Schorr

Pride: The Story of Harvey Milk and the Rainbow Flag by Rob Sanders, illustrated by Steven Salerno

PODCAST
Making Gay History